PINTEREST MARKETING WORKBOOK:

HOW TO USE PINTEREST

FOR BUSINESS

2016 EDITION

BY JASON MCDONALD, PH.D.

© 2015-2016, JM INTERNET GROUP

https://www.jm-seo.org/

Tel. 800-298-4065

0

INTRODUCTION

Welcome to the *Pinterest Marketing Workbook, 2016 edition*! Get ready to

- have some **fun**;
- **learn how Pinterest works;**
- understand how to use **Pinterest** to **market your business**; and
- create a step-by-step **Pinterest marketing plan**.

Fully revised and updated for 2016, this workbook not only explains how to market on Pinterest but also provides access to **free** Pinterest marketing tools. It provides overviews, step-by-step instructions, tips and secrets, free tools for Pinterest marketing, and (*wait, there's more!*) access to worksheets that will help you build a systematic Pinterest marketing plan. Even better, if you register your copy, you also get access to my complete *Social Media Toolbook*, with literally hundreds of free social media marketing tools to turbocharge your social media marketing not just on Pinterest but also on LinkedIn, Twitter, Facebook, Google+, YouTube, Instagram and other major social media platforms.

> *It slices, it dices. It explains how to Pinterest works. It gives you free tools. And it helps you make a Pinterest marketing plan.*

If you're really gung-ho for **social media marketing**, I refer you to my *Social Media Workbook*, an all-in-one guide to the entire social media universe from Pinterest to LinkedIn, Twitter to Facebook, Instagram to YouTube, Yelp to Google+, and everything in between. Learn more about that book at http://jmlinks.com/social or call 800-298-4065.

Why Market via Pinterest?

If you've read this far, you're definitely intrigued by Pinterest as a marketing platform. Perhaps you're just starting out with a **Pinterest Account** for your **business**. Or perhaps you already have an Account, but want to make it really work. Let's step back for a minute and ask: **why market on Pinterest**?

Here are some reasons:

- **Pinterest is pro-shopping.** People use Pinterest as an "idea board" system, and much of that is shopping-related. Pinterest users, therefore, are very receptive to marketing messages, especially in retail and do-it-yourself topics.
- **Pinterest is growing rapidly.** Pinterest has been one of the most rapidly growing social media, and with a strong foothold in women and shopping, it has room to grow upwards to new demographics and new usages. The Pinterest train has not yet left the station!
- **Pinterest is Unique.** The concept of "pins" and "idea boards" was invented by Pinterest, and as a visual bookmarking system makes Pinterest different from all other social media. Indeed, in a desperate struggle to remain relevant, Google+ has copied Pinterest with its "collections" concept.
- **Pinterest is cheap**. Pinterest is, of course, free to use. And in terms of marketing there is a lot you can do, for free, to build your brand, spread eWOM (electronic word of mouth), help you stay top-of-mind with your customers, and even "get shares" or "go viral." Pinterest can work hand in glove with your online eCommerce store.
- **Pinterest has advertising.** If you advertise smart on Pinterest, and combine paid advertising with free organic Pinterest marketing, you can grow the reach of your company via promoted pins.

Pinterest, however, is also complicated. Using it is one thing, and marketing on Pinterest is another. Most businesses fail at Pinterest marketing because they just don't "get it." They don't understand how Pinterest works, especially the concepts of "idea boards" and "pins," and they fail to see the incredible marketing opportunities beneath the surface of recipes, do-it-yourself knitting projects, and the disorder of the Pinterest visual bookmarking system. Others focus on Pinterest, without really seeing that to-date it has a narrow range on retail, women, and do-it-yourselfers. Quite simply, you have to invest some time to learn whether and/or "how" to market on Pinterest.

Enter the *Pinterest Marketing Workbook*.

Who is this Workbook For?

This workbook is aimed primarily at **small business owners** and **marketing managers**. Non-profits will also find it useful.

If you are a person whose job involves advertising, marketing, and/or branding, this workbook is for you. If you are a small business that sees a marketing opportunity in Pinterest, this workbook is for you. And if your job is to market a business or organization online in today's Internet economy, this book is for you. Anyone who wants to look behind the curtain and understand the mechanics of how to market on Pinterest will benefit from this book.

Anyone who sees – however dimly – that Pinterest could help market their business will benefit from this hands-on guide. Anyone in retail, do-it-yourself (crafts or hobbies), or the female shopping demographic should be crazy excited for Pinterest!

How Does This Workbook Work?

This workbook starts first with an overview to **social media *marketing***. If social media is a **party**, then **using social media** is akin to just *showing up*. **Marketing** on social media, in contrast, isn't about showing up. It's about ***throwing*** the party!

Understanding that distinction between "attending" the social media party and "throwing" the social media party is the subject of **Chapter One.**

Chapter Two is a deep dive into Pinterest marketing. We'll overview how Pinterest works, explain everything from idea boards to pins, comments to shares, and explore how to search Pinterest. It will all become much clearer, as we work through Pinterest in plain English, written for "mere mortals." Along the way, I'll provide **worksheets** that will act as "Jason as therapist," so you can fill them out and begin to outline your own unique Pinterest marketing plan.

Finally, this workbook ends with an **Appendix**: a list of amazing **free Pinterest tools** and resources. Even better, if you register your copy, you get clickable online access to the tools, a PDF copy of the book, and (wait, there's more!) a complimentary copy of my *Social Media Toolbook*, my compilation of hundreds of social media tools not just for Pinterest but for all the major platforms.

Here's how to register your copy of this workbook:

1. Go to https://jm-seo.org/workbooks
2. Click on Pinterest.
3. Use this password: **pinterest2016**

4. You're in. Simply click on the link for a PDF copy of the *Social Media Toolbook* as well as access to the worksheets referenced herein.

OK, now that we know what this workbook is about, who it is for, and our plan of action...

Let's get started!

≫ MEET THE AUTHOR

My name is Jason McDonald, and I have been active on the Internet since 1994 (having invented the Internet along with Al Gore) and taught SEO, AdWords, and Social Media since 2009 – online, at Stanford University Continuing Studies, at both AcademyX and the Bay Area Video Coalition in San Francisco, at workshops, and in corporate trainings across these United States. I love figuring out how things work, and I love teaching others! Social media marketing is an endeavor that I understand, and I want to empower you to understand it as well.

Learn more about me at https://www.jasonmcdonald.org/ or at my corporate website https://www.jm-seo.org/. Or just call 800-298-4065, say something flattering, and I my secretary will put you through. *(Like I have a secretary! Just call if you have something to ask or say).*

≫ SPREAD THE WORD: WRITE A REVIEW & GET A FREE EBOOK!

If you like this workbook, please take a moment to write an honest review on Amazon.com. *If you hate the book, feel free to trash it on Amazon or anywhere across the Internet. (I have thick skin). If you hate life, in general, and are just one of those bitter people who write bitter reviews... well, gosh, go off and meditate, talk to a priest or do something spiritual. Life is just too short to be that bitter!*

At any rate, here is my special offer for those lively enough to write a review of the book–

1. Write your **honest review** on Amazon.com.
2. **Contact** me via https://www.jm-seo.org/contact and let me know your review is up.

3. Include your **email address** and **website URL**, and any quick questions you have about it.
4. I will send you a **free** copy of one of my other eBooks which cover AdWords, SEO, and Social Media Marketing.

This offer is limited to the first 100 reviewers, and only for reviewers who have purchased a paid copy of the book. You may be required to show proof of purchase and the birth certificate of your first born child, cat, or goldfish. If you don't have a child, cat, or goldfish, you may be required to prove telepathically that you bought the book.

>> QUESTIONS AND MORE INFORMATION

I **encourage** my students to ask questions! If you have questions, submit them via https://www.jm-seo.org/contact/. There are two sorts of questions: ones that I know instantly, for which I'll zip you an email answer right away, and ones I do not know instantly, in which case I will investigate and we'll figure out the answer together.

As a teacher, I learn most from my students. So please don't be shy!

>> COPYRIGHT AND DISCLAIMER

Uh! Legal stuff! Get ready for some fun:

This is a completely **unofficial** guide to Pinterest marketing. Pinterest has endorsed this guide, nor has anyone affiliated with Pinterest been involved in the production of this guide.

That's a *good thing*. This guide is **independent**. My aim is to "tell it as I see it," giving you no-nonsense information on how to succeed at Pinterest marketing.

In addition, please note the following:

- All trademarks are the property of their respective owners. I have no relationship with nor endorsement from the mark holders. Any use of their marks is so I can provide information to you.

- Any reference to or citation of third party products or services whether for Pinterest, LinkedIn, Twitter, Yelp, Google / Google+, Yahoo, Bing, YouTube, Facebook, or other businesses, search engines, or social media platforms, should not be construed as an endorsement of those products or services tools, nor as a warranty as to their effectiveness or compliance with the terms of service with any search engine or social media platform.

The information used in this guide was derived in August, 2015. However, social media marketing changes rapidly, so please be aware that scenarios, facts, and conclusions are subject to change without notice.

Additional Disclaimer. Internet marketing is an art, and not a science. Any changes to your Internet marketing strategy, including SEO, Social Media Marketing, and AdWords, is at your own risk. Neither Jason McDonald, Excerpti Communications, Inc., nor the JM Internet Group assumes any responsibility for the effect of any changes you may, or may not, make to your website or AdWords advertising based on the information in this guide.

» ACKNOWLEDGEMENTS

No man is an island. I would like to thank my beloved wife, Noelle Decambra, for helping me hand-in-hand as the world's best moderator for our online classes, and as my personal cheerleader in the book industry. Gloria McNabb has done her usual tireless job as first assistant, including updating this edition as well the *Social Media Marketing* toolbook. Alex Facklis and Hannah McDonald also assisted with tools and research. I would also like to thank my black Labrador retriever, Buddy, for countless walks and games of fetch, during which I refined my ideas about marketing and about life.

And, again, a huge thank you to my students – online, in San Francisco, and at Stanford Continuing Studies. You challenge me, you inspire me, and you motivate me!

PARTY ON

Most books on **social media marketing** (or **SMM** for short) either focus on the high, high level of hype, hype, hype or focus on the low, low, low level of micro technical details. It's either Malcolm Gladwell's *Blink*, Seth Godin's *Purple Cow*, David Meerman Scott's *The New Rules of Marketing and PR* – or it's *Social Media for Dummies*, *LinkedIn for Dummies*, or *Teach Yourself Facebook in Ten Minutes*.

You're either up in the sky, or lost in the weeds.

This book is different: it focuses on the middle, productive ground – part **theory**, and part **practice**. It gives you a framework for how to "think" about social media marketing as well as concrete advice on how to "do" social media marketing on Pinterest in particular.

Throughout, it provides worksheets, videos, Todos and deliverables, to help you create a step-by-step social media marketing plan as well as a step-by-step Pinterest marketing plan. Used in combination with the *Social Media Toolbook*, which identifies hundreds of **free** tools for social media marketing all in one convenient place, small business owners and marketers finally have a practical, hands-on method for practical social media marketing.

This first chapter is about *how to think about social media marketing*. What is social media marketing? Why are you doing it? What should you do, step-by-step, to succeed?

Let's get started!

TO DO LIST:

> » Understand that Social Media Marketing is Like Throwing a Party

> » Recognize the Social Media Marketing Illusion

> » Identify Relevant Discovery Paths

>> Establish Goals and KPIs

>> Remember the Big Picture

>> Deliverable: a "Big Picture" Social Media Marketing Plan

>> UNDERSTAND THAT SOCIAL MEDIA MARKETING IS LIKE THROWING A PARTY

Have you ever **attended** a party? You know, received an invitation, showed up, said hello and various meets and greets to other guests, ate the *yummy yummy* food, drank the liquor (or the diet soda), hobnobbed with other guests, ate some more food, danced the night away, thanked the hosts, and left?

> *Attending* a party is all about *showing up*, *enjoying* the entertainment and food, and *leaving*.

Have you ever **used** Twitter? Facebook? Instagram? You know, logged in, checked out some funny accounts, read some posts, posted back and forth with friends and family, checked your updates, and then logged out?

That's *attending* a party. That's *using* social media.

> *Using* social media is all about *logging in*, *enjoying* what's new and exciting, and *logging out*.

Throwing a party, however, is something entirely different from **attending** a party. Similarly, **marketing** via social media is something entirely different from **using** social media.

This chapter explores the basics of social media *marketing*: of **throwing** the "social media party" vs. just **showing up**. That word *marketing* is very important: we're exploring how to use social media to enhance our brand, grow the visibility of our company, product or service, or even (gasp!) use social media to sell more stuff.

PARTY ON: BECOME A

GREAT PARTY-THROWER

Social media marketing is the art and science of throwing "great parties" on Twitter, Facebook, LinkedIn, Pinterest and the like in such a way that people not only show up to enjoy the party but also are primed to buy your product or service.

Let's explore this analogy further: how is social media *marketing* like *throwing a party*?

Here are three ways:

Invitations. A great party needs great guests, and the first step to getting guests is to identify an attendee list, and send out invitations. Who will be invited? How will we invite them – will it be by phone call, email, postal mail, etc.? For your social media marketing, you'll need to identify your target audience(s) and brainstorm how to get them to "show up" on your social media page via tactics like sending out emails, cross-posting your Facebook to your Twitter, or your LinkedIn to your blog, advertising, or even using "real world" face-to-face invitations like "Hey, follow us on Twitter to get coupons and insider deals."

Social media marketing requires having a promotion strategy.

Entertainment. Will your party have a band, a magician, a comedian, or just music? What is your entertainment strategy? What kind of food will you serve: Mexican, Chinese, Tapas, or something else? Similarly for your social media marketing: why will people "hang out" on your Facebook page or YouTube channel? Will it be to learn something? Will it be because it's fun or funny?

Social media marketing requires having a content marketing strategy, a way to systematically produce yummy yummy content (blog posts, infographics, images, videos) that people will enjoy enough to "hang out" on your social media page or channel.

Hosting. As the host of your party, you'll "hang out" at the party, but while the guests are busy enjoying themselves, you'll be busy, meeting and greeting, making sure everything is running smoothly, and doing other behind-the-scenes tasks. Similarly, in your social media marketing, you'll be busy coordinating content, interacting with guests and even policing the party to "kick out" rude or obnoxious guests.

Social media marketing requires behind-the-scenes management, often on a day-to-day basis, to ensure that everything is running

SOCIAL MEDIA MARKETING IS

THROWING A PARTY

Oh, and one more thing. Let's assume, for example, you're going to throw your wife an amazing 40th birthday party. Before that party, you'll probably start attending other parties with a critical eye – noting what you like, and what you don't like, what you want to imitate, and even reaching out to the magicians, bands, and bartenders to find out what they cost and possibly hire them for your own party.

You'll "inventory" other parties and make a list of likes and dislikes, ideas and do-not-dos, and use that information to systematically plan your own party.

As a social media marketer, therefore, you should "attend" the parties of other brands online. Identify brands you like (REI, Whole Foods, Father Robert Barron), "follow" or "like" them, and keep a critical eye on what they're doing. **Inventory** your likes and dislikes, and **reverse engineer** what other marketers are up to. And in your industry, do the same: follow companies in your own industry, again with the goal of "reverse engineering" their social media marketing strategy, successes, and failures.

For your first TODO, identify some brands you admire and "follow" them on Twitter, LinkedIn, Facebook, Pinterest etc. Start making a list of what you like, or dislike, based on reverse engineering their online marketing strategy. Become a good user of social media, but with an eye to the marketing strategy "behind the scenes."

» RECOGNIZE THE SOCIAL MEDIA MARKETING ILLUSION

Successful social media is based on **illusion**, just like successful parties are based on illusion.

How so?

Let's think for a second about an amazing party. Think back to a holiday party you attended, a great birthday or graduation party, or even a corporate event. Was it fun? Did it seem magical? It probably did.

Now, if you've ever had the (mis)fortune of planning such an event – what was that like? Was it fun? Was it magical? Yes and no, but it was also probably a lot of work, "in the background," to make sure that the party ran smoothly.

Great parties have an element of **illusion** in them: they *seem* effortless, while *in reality* (behind the scenes) an incredible amount of strategy, planning, and hard work goes on. Similarly, great social media marketing efforts (*think Katy Perry or Lady Gaga on social media, think Whole Foods on social media, or REI, Zappos, Burt's Bees, or even Nutella*), create an illusion. They (only) "seem" spontaneous, they (only) "seem" effortless. But in the background a ton of work is going on to promote, manage, and grow these "social media parties."

ILLUSION IS COMMON TO GREAT PARTIES AND GREAT SOCIAL MEDIA MARKETING

With respect to social media marketing, this illusion often creates a weird problem for you vis-a-vis upper management or the boss. Upper management or your boss might mistakenly believe that "social media is easy," and/or "social media is free." You, as the marketer, might have to educate your boss that it only "looks" easy, or "seems" free. Social media marketing requires a ton of strategy, hard work, and (gasp!) even money or sweat equity to make it happen. Among your early tasks at social media marketing may be to explain the "social media marketing" illusion to your boss. It only seems easy. It only seems free.

For your second TODO, organize a meeting with your boss and/or marketing team. Discuss all the things that have to get done to be successful at social media marketing, ranging from conducting an **inventory** of competitor efforts, to **setting up basic accounts** on Twitter, Facebook, LinkedIn, etc., to **creating content** to share on social media (images, photos, blog posts, infographics, videos), to **monitoring** social media channels on an on-going basis, and finally to **measuring** your successes. Educate the team that although it might not take a lot of money, social media marketing does take significant amount of work!

We're planning an awesome party here, people. It's going to take a ton of work, it's going to be a ton of fun, and it's going to be incredibly successful!

Now, don't get discouraged. *Please don't get discouraged.* As marketers, we are so fortunate to live in an amazing time with incredible new opportunities to reach our target customers.

- Is social media free? Yes (and no).
- Is it effortless? No.
- Is it worth it? Yes, yes, yes!

Social media marketing takes a lot of hard work, and it can be incredible. *Don't get discouraged!*

Know the Question and Find the Answer

Oh, and once you start to view social media marketing as a systematic process, a great thing will happen: you'll formulate concrete, specific questions. And, once you know a question you can find the answer.

Once you realize, for example, that Facebook allows cover photos, and that great Facebook marketers swap theirs out from time to time, you can create the "questions" of how do you create a cover photo for Facebook, what are the dimensions, etc.

IF YOU KNOW THE QUESTION, YOU CAN FIND THE ANSWER.

As you begin your social media marketing efforts, once you "know a question," simply go to Google to "find the answer." For example, simply Google "What are the dimensions of a Facebook cover photo" to end up on the Facebook help site or other websites that will tell you the answer. You now realize a) you need a series of compelling Facebook cover photos for your page, b) there are specific dimensions and policies required by Facebook, and c) either you or someone on your team has the "task" of making this happen on a regular basis.

» IDENTIFY RELEVANT DISCOVERY PATHS

Before we plunge into Facebook, Twitter, and the gang, it's worthwhile to sit back and ponder the big questions of marketing. What do you sell? Who wants it and why? And, very directly: how do customers find you?

This last one might seem like a simple question, but a great social marketer has a very specific understanding of the paths by which customers find her product, service, or company. This understanding then guides -

> *How much should you focus on SEO (Search Engine Optimization)? How much should you focus on AdWords? How much on Facebook? Or Twitter? Should you buy ads on Television, or (gasp!) send out unsolicited email (spam)? Is Pinterest worth the effort?*

Once you brainstorm how customers find you, you will have a fundamental understanding of how to construct a systematic social media marketing plan.

Fortunately, there are only five paths of customer discovery. Only five. Every way that someone finds a product or service can be categorized by the following five **discovery paths**.

Search. The search path occurs when the customer is "searching" for a company, product, or service. For example, a customer is hungry. He types into Google or Yelp, "pizza." He browses available restaurants, chooses one, and shows up to get pizza. *He searched for pizza. He found pizza. He made a decision.* The search path is the province of SEO (Search Engine Optimization), largely on Google but also on sites such as Yelp that work via "keywords" to help customers find stuff that they want.

Review / Recommend / Trust. The review / recommend /trust path is based on "trust indicators." In it, the customer already has created a list of vendors he or she might use, but he is researching "whom to trust." In this path, he might use the "reviews" and/or "stars" on Yelp or Google as "trust indicators" to predict which pizza restaurant is good (or bad). Reviews and stars are the most common trust indicators in social media marketing, but having a robust Facebook page, with many followers and interesting posts can also be a "trust indicator." Having an expert-looking profile on LinkedIn can be a "trust indicator" for a CPA or an architect. A recommendation from a friend or colleague also plays into reviews and trust.

eWOM / Share / Viral. Wow! That pizza was great! Let me take a selfie of me chowing down on the pizza, and post it to Instagram. Look friends: it's me, chowing down on pizza, having fun, livin' the life, while you're back in the dorm studying. Or, hey, Facebook friends, do you know of a great place to host a kid's birthday party? You do (electronic word of mouth). Or, wow, here is a cat video of cats at the pizza restaurant puzzled by the self-serve soda fountain. It's "gone viral" on YouTube and has sixteen million views! The share path occurs when a customer loves the product, service, or experience enough to "share" it on social media – be that via electronic word of mouth, a share on his or her Facebook page, a "selfie" on Instagram, or a viral video on YouTube.

Interrupt. The interrupt path is the bad boy of online marketing. Interrupt marketing occurs when you want to watch a YouTube video but before you can watch it *five, four, three, two, one,* you have to view an annoying ad. Or, when you get a spam email on "amazing Viagra." Interrupt is largely used in advertising, and largely used to "push" products that people aren't proactively looking for.

Browse. The browse path is a little similar to the interrupt path. In it, you're looking for something, reading something, or watching something, and alongside comes something else. For example, you go to YouTube to look up "how to tie a tie," and in the suggested videos at the end is a video for Dollar Shave Club. Or you see Dollar Shave Club videos suggested at the right of the screen. You're not proactively looking for Dollar Shave Club, but you see their information as you "browse" for related content on sites like YouTube, Facebook, or blogs.

First and foremost, social media marketing excels at the **share** path. Getting customers to share your product or service is, in many ways, the Holy Grail of social media marketing. But the Search path, the eWOM / Trust / Recommend path, and the Browse path are all also important.

For your third Todo, download the **Big Picture Marketing worksheet**. For the worksheet, go to *https://www.jm-seo.org/workbooks* (click on Pinterest, enter the code 'pinterest2016' to register if you have not already done so), and click on the link to the "Big Picture Marketing."

In this worksheet, you'll write a "business value proposition" explaining what you sell, and who are the target customers. You'll also identify the most relevant "discovery paths" by which potential customers find your products. That in turn, will get you to start thinking about which media are the most relevant to your online marketing efforts.

» Establish Goals and KPIs (Key Performance Indicators)

Marketing is about measurement. Are we helping our brand image? Are we encouraging sales? How do we know where we are succeeding, and where there is more work to be done? Why are we spending all this blood, sweat, and tears on social media marketing anyway?

In today's overhyped social media environment, many marketers feel like they "must" be on Twitter, or they "must" have a presence on Pinterest. All of the social media companies – Facebook, Twitter, Pinterest, Yelp – have a vested interest in overhyping the importance of their platform, and using fear to compel marketers to "not miss out" by massively jumping on the latest and greatest social platform. Social media guilt, however, is to be avoided: if you define a clear business value proposition, know where your customers are, and establish clear goals and KPIs (Key Performance Indicators), you'll be able to focus on those social platforms that really help you and ignore the ones that are just hype.

Avoid social media guilt: you can't (and shouldn't) do everything

Let's identify some common goals for effective social media marketing. The boss might have an ultimate "hard" goal of getting sales leads or selling stuff online. Those are definitely important, but as marketers, we might look to intermediary or "soft goals" such as nurturing a positive brand image online or growing our online reviews.

Generally speaking, social media excels at the "soft goals" of growing brand awareness, nurturing customer conversations, encouraging reviews and the like and is not so good at immediate, direct goals like lead captures or sales.

In any case, having high-level yet soft goals is essential to being able to create a systematic, social media marketing strategy as well as a "drilldown" strategy for an individual social medium, whether that be Twitter or LinkedIn, Instagram or YouTube.

Here are common goals for social media marketing:

> **eWOM (electronic Word of Mouth).** Every brand wants people to talk about it in a positive way, and today a lot of that conversation occurs on social media. If we're a local pizza restaurant, we want people "talking" about us on Yelp, on Facebook, on Twitter as a great place to get pizza, eat Italian food, cater a wedding, or host a birthday party for little Jimmy. As marketers, a common goal for social media is to grow and nurture positive eWOM, which might be positive

conversations on Facebook, positive reviews on Yelp or Google+ local, relationships between us and customers and among customers, and the sharing of our brand across media.

Customer Continuum. *A prospect becomes a customer, a customer becomes a fan, and a fan becomes an evangelist.* For example, I'm hungry. I search for "great pizza" in Palo Alto, California, and I find your pizza restaurant. I try your pizza, thereby becoming a customer. It's good, and I'm a fan: if someone asks me, I'll recommend Jason's Palo Alto Pizza. And finally, I love your pizza so much, I wrote a positive review on Yelp, I created a YouTube video of me eating your pizza, and I have a new blog on Tumblr about your pizza. As marketers, we want to encourage customers to move to the right on the customer continuum: from prospect to customer, customer to fan, and fan to evangelist. We are also aware of (and seek to mitigate) the "customer from hell" who can hate a brand so much that she writes a negative review on Yelp, posts negative comments on Facebook, or creates a viral YouTube about your terrible pizza (**reputation management**).

Trust Indicators. We want pizza. We look at reviews. We use reviews to decide which pizza restaurant is probably good. We want to go to a theme park. We look at their Facebook page. We choose the one that looks active, that looks like people are having fun. Trust indicators are all about mental "short cuts" that customers make to identify possible vendors, services, or products. A common goal of social media marketing, therefore, is to nurture positive trust indicators about our brand online: reviews, especially but not only.

One Touch to Many. You visit the pizza restaurant, one time. As a marketer, I want to convert that "one touch" to "many." I want you to follow us on Twitter, so I can Tweet special deals, promotions, what's cooking, and stay "top of mind," so that when you're hungry again, you think, Jason's Palo Alto Pizza. Using social media to convert one touch to many and stay top of mind is an excellent goal.

Promotion, promotion, promotion. Social sharing – getting customers to market your brand – is probably the most common social media goal. I want you to Instagram you and your kids having a great pizza party! I want you to share our amazing corporate catering event with your Facebook friends. Encouraging social sharing / eWOM / viral marketing is a huge, huge goal for SMM.

Social Media Marketing excels at the "soft goals" listed above. Note, in particular the desired "virtuous circle" of social media.

The more positive reviews I have on Yelp, the most customers I get, the most customers I get, the more positive reviews. The more followers on Twitter I get, the more chances I have to get them to share my discounts, the most discounts they share, the more followers I get. The more people like / share / comment on my Facebook page, the better my Edgerank (a measurement of how engaging one's content is), the better my Edgerank, the more people see my content, the more people see my content, the more shares I get on Facebook, the better my Edgerank.

NURTURE A VIRTUOUS CIRCLE

Nurturing a virtuous circle is a major, major goal of an effective social media marketing system. And finally, don't forget, that in most cases we want all of these "soft goals" to turn into "hard goals": a positive brand image to lead to more sales, and a stronger bottom line.

For your fourth TODO, download the **Marketing Goals Worksheet**. For the worksheet, go to *https://www.jm-seo.org/workbooks* (click on Pinterest, enter the code 'pinterest2016' to register if you have not already done so), and click on the link to the "Marketing Goals Marketing."

In this worksheet, you'll identify your "hard" goals, whether you have something "free" to offer, and your "soft" goals on social media. Ultimately, these big picture goals will be translated into much more specific goals, germane to a social medium such as YouTube, Twitter, or Facebook.

≫ ESTABLISH A CONTENT MARKETING SYSTEM

Bring on the chips! Carry out the diet coke! Turn on the band! A great party needs great food and great entertainment: these are the "fuel" of the successful party. Similarly, great social media marketing needs the "fuel" of content: interesting (funny, shocking, outrageous, sentimental) blog posts, images, photographs, infographics and instructographics, memes and even videos that will make it worthwhile to "subscribe" to your social channel (like / follow / circle) and keep coming back for more.

To succeed at social media marketing you must succeed at **content marketing**. You gotta gotta gotta create a system for identifying and creating interesting content to share via your social networks. Among the most commonly shared items are:

Images. Photographs and images are the bread-and-butter of Facebook, Instagram, and even Twitter.

Memes. From grumpy cat to success kid, memes make the funny and memorable, sticky and shareable on social media.

Infographics and Instructographics. From how to tie a tie to sixteen ways you can help stop global warming, people love to read and share pictures that tell a story, hopefully with facts.

Blog Posts. An oldie but goodie: an informative, witty, funny, informational, or fact-filled post about a topic that matters to your customers.

Slide Shows. From Slideshare to just posting your PowerPoints online, a hybrid visual and textual cornucopia of social sharing fun.

Videos. If a picture tells a thousand words, a video can tell ten thousand. YouTube is a social medium in its own right, but the videos themselves are content that can be enjoyed and shared.

In sum, you'll need fuel to power your social media marketing. This fuel comes in two main varieties: other people's content, and your own content. The advantage of the former is that it is easy to get, while the advantage of the latter is that because it's yours, you control the message. The disadvantage of other people's content is that you do not control the message (and it thereby promotes them to some extent), while the disadvantage of your own content is that its takes time and effort to produce.

To be an effective social sharer, you need both: **other people's content** and **your own content**.

Your goal is to position yourself (your company, your CEO, your brand) as a "useful expert," the "goto" person or brand that people come to to find interesting and useful stuff in your market ecosystem. My own brand, for example, at *https://www.jasonmcdonald.org/* is all about sharing interesting, fun, and useful stuff on social media, AdWords, and SEO. That's why I have over 7,000 followers on Google+: because I'm useful.

Other People's Content

Fortunately, there are tools to help you systematically identify and share other people's content. (All are listed in the *Social Media Toolbook*, content marketing section). Here are some of my favorites:

Buzzsumo (*http://buzzsumo.com*) - Buzzsumo is a 'buzz' monitoring tool for social media. Input a website (domain) and/or a topic and see what people are sharing across Facebook, Twitter, Google+ and other social media. Great for link-building (because what people link to is what they share), and also for social media.

Topsy (*http://topsy.com*) - Real-time Twitter search engine. You can also search the web and videos. VERY important: you can input a URL, e.g., jm-seo.org or chipestimate.com, and see how frequently that URL and its sub URLs have been tweeted. Great way to see your social shares as well as discover what's trending on the blogosphere for more effective blogging.

Feedly (*http://feedly.com*) - Feedly is a newsreader integrated with Google+ or Facebook. It's useful for social media because you can follow important blogs or other content and share it with your followers. It can also spur great blog ideas.

Easely (*http://easel.ly*) - Use thousands of templates and design objects to easily create infographics for your blog. A competitor is Piktochart (*http://piktochart.com*).

Meme Generator (*http://memegenerator.net*) - Memes are shareable photos, usually with text. But how do you create them? Why, use memegenerator.net.

In terms of other people's content, you want to first identify the "themes" of social media about which you want to talk. An expert in tax issues, for example, might monitor California tax law, small business, and individual tax shelter issues. He can then systematically monitor them via a tool such as Feedly, and use Feedly to easily share other people's content across his social networks. A Palo Alto pizza restaurant might monitor content on the San Francisco Bay Area as well as pizza / italian food, and ideas for wedding catering and birthday parties. By being a "helpful sharer" of this information, the pizza restaurant can stay "top of mind" by providing useful content to people planning corporate events, weddings, and birthday parties as well as looking for fun things to do in the Bay Area.

Your Own Content

For your own content, the steps are to first brainstorm a useful content idea (e.g., an infographic on common ways for small business owners to save on taxes, or sixteen ways weddings can go terribly wrong), second to create it in whatever format you want (image, infographic, blog post, video), and third to share it across your relevant social networks. For managing your posts across social networks, I highly recommend Hootsuite (*https://www.hootsuite.com/*), which is a cloud-based social media management tool.

For your final TODO, download and complete the **Content Marketing Worksheet**. For the worksheet, go to *https://www.jm-seo.org/workbooks* (click on Pinterest, enter the code 'pinterest2016' to register if you have not already done so), and click on the link to the "Content Marketing Worksheet."

For a great list of the top ten tools for content marketing, please visit *http://jmlinks.com/2h*.

» REMEMBER THE BIG PICTURE

At this point, you've begun your social media marketing journey. You've understood that social media marketing is about "throwing" the party more than "attending the party." You've realized you need to start "paying attention" with regard to what other marketers are doing on social media, with an eye to "reverse engineering" their marketing strategy so that you have ideas of what you like, and do not like, in terms of social media. You've started to brainstorm "discovery paths" and "goals" for your SMM efforts.

And you've realized that once you've identified your goals, identified relevant social media, set up your social accounts, the really hard work will be a) promoting your social media channels, and b) creating the kind of content that makes them want to "like you," keep coming back for more, and share your message with their friends, family, and/or business colleagues.

You've understood that **promotion** and **content creation** are the big on-going tasks of successful social media marketing.

» DELIVERABLE: OUTLINE A SOCIAL MEDIA MARKETING PLAN

Now that we've come to the end of Chapter 1, your first DELIVERABLE has arrived. For the worksheet, go to *https://www.jm-seo.org/workbooks* (click on Pinterest, enter the code 'pinterest2016' to register if you have not already done so), and click on the link to the "Social Media Marketing Plan Big Picture Worksheet." By filling out this plan, you and your team will establish a vision of what you want to achieve via social media marketing.

Now it's time to drill into individual media, starting with Pinterest, the 24/7 idea-generating, pin-pinning, pro-shopping, do-it-yourselfer, dreaming, visual bookmarking system that's a favorite with females, do-it-yourselfers, and dreamers of all types. Let's get started!

2

PINTEREST

Some social media like Facebook, YouTube, and LinkedIn are broad, reaching many people with many diverse interests. Others are narrow, reaching only specific people (demographic groups like *young people* or *women*, for example) or specific usages (e.g., *plumbing*, *restaurants*, *dentistry*, etc., for example). Yelp, Tumblr, Instagram, Twitter, and Pinterest fall into this latter category. They are very strong in the niches, but not so strong in the generalities. If your specific customer segment or usage is active on the particular social media, it works wonders. If not, not.

> Pinterest is such a platform: incredibly strong in **retail** and the **female demographic**, and all but absent from nearly everything else.

Pinterest focuses its marketing strengths on three intertwined segments: **consumer retail**, **do-it-yourself**, and **women**. Shoppers use Pinterest to browse the Internet and "pin" items they might want to buy to "boards." Do-it-yourselfers use Pinterest to share ideas on how to build this or that, knit this or that, or construct this or that. Women, always a heavy shopping demographic, have been the early adopters of Pinterest both as a "buying / idea platform" and as a great platform for do-it-yourself crafting and recipe-sharing.

Pinterest, in short, is *the* network for consumer retail, *the* network for craftsy do-it-yourself, and *the* network for women (especially in shopping mode).

Why consider Pinterest? Here's a recap.

First and foremost, Pinterest is about shopping. Consumers use it as an "idea board" for their college dorm room, their wedding, the doggie toys they want to make or buy, their house redecorating project, their recipe ideas for their next family reunion. The site makes it easy to "pin" ideas to a "board," and each pin can be instantly clickable to a blog post or online store where a person can learn more, or (gasp!) buy the item. The ROI from Pinterest can be very high because consumers are often in a buying mindset then they use the platform! Do-it-yourself is also very big on Pinterest; but let's face it, people often see "do-it-yourself" and then "buy" related products. Second, the unique "idea board" system makes Pinterest a wonderful mechanism for collaboration among customers, and between you and your customers. If an idea has a visual component, Pinterest may prove to be a wonderful way to share and brainstorm that idea. Third, Pinterest is highly visual and can act as a bookmarking system, whether social or not. Once you get the hang of it, you may fall in love with Pinterest just for its bookmarking capabilities alone.

Let's get started!

TO DO LIST:

>> Explore how Pinterest Works

>> Inventory Companies on Pinterest

>> Set up and Optimize Your Account

>> Brainstorm and Execute a Pinning Strategy

>> Promote Your Pinterest Account, Boards, and Pins

>> Measure your Results

>> Deliverable: a Pinterest Marketing Plan

>> Appendix: Top Ten Pinterest Marketing Tools and Resources

>> EXPLORE HOW PINTEREST WORKS

The best way to understand Pinterest and social bookmarking is to grasp the concept of an "idea board."

Let's use the example of someone planning out her ideal dorm room for freshman year at college. First, she signs up for Pinterest and creates a profile. Compared with Facebook, Pinterest is very basic: not a lot of information is displayed in a Pinterest profile, pretty much just a profile picture and a very brief description. Next, she should download and install the Pinterest button (see *http://jmlinks.com/2m*) or Chrome Pinterest extension (see *http://jmlinks.com/2n*). Once installed, she can now surf the Web (or use the Pinterest app for iPhone or Android) and "pin" interesting items to "boards" that she sets up.

For example, she'd set up a board "my dream college room" or even more specific boards like "my dream bathroom supplies," or "my dream desk." Let's say she goes to Amazon and finds an amazing desk light. She can "pin" this desk light to her "dream desk" board. People who follow her (or this board) on Pinterest, thus see this desk light in their Pinterest news feed, whereupon they can comment on it and (gasp!) and even buy it for her. And of course, she would pin not just one desk light, but several possible desk lights, several pencil holders, several ink pads, a few art posters for above her desk, and on and on. It's as if she's building a collage of desk possibilities, from which she can select the perfect accessories. As she creates idea boards for her dream desk, dream closet, dream door room, and dream bathroom supplies, she can invite her friends, her Mom, her sorority sisters to collaborate by commenting and pinning to the boards as well. Pinterest, in short, is a visual bookmarking and idea board system, one that can be social as well, and one that makes online shopping as easy as discover, click, buy. People also use it before purchase in the real world, as a social scrapbook to group together products and services they might want to buy at a brick and mortar store. And do-it-yourselfers use it to share ideas about how to build this or that, how to cook this or that.

THE ESSENCE OF PINTEREST IS THE IDEA BOARD

The structure of Pinterest in a nutshell is:

Individual profile: me, Jason as a person.

Idea board: collections of items from the Web on topics like my "dream dorm room," "dog toys to possibly buy," "do-it-yourself Christmas decorations," or "recipes for summer parties."

Pins: I can "pin" things I find on the Web such as blog posts, videos, images, or products to buy to my "boards" as a collection of ideas, things to buy. I can also upload items directly.

Search. I can browse Pinterest, search Pinterest, or search the Web for interesting things to "pin" to my boards.

Collaboration: I can invite others to comment on my board or pins, and to pin items to my boards directly. I can also pin things to their boards.

Social: I have a news feed, wherein Pinterest shows me the pins of people, brands, and boards I follow as well as suggestions based on my (revealed) interests. People can also follow me and my boards, and like, comment, and reshare items that I am pinning. Through collaborative boards, we can pin and share ideas together.

To get the hang of Pinterest, create your personal profile, create some boards, download the "Pin it" button, and start playing with the site. Using Pinterest is the best way to begin to understand how to market on Pinterest. For example, to view a Pinterest search for "dream college dorm rooms," visit *http://jmlinks.com/2o*. To visit some sample idea boards, visit *http://jmlinks.com/2p*. Notice how people use Pinterest as a visual bookmarking system of ideas (largely, but not exclusively, of stuff to buy or make), and how others can comment on, and even contribute to these boards in a collaborative fashion.

Pay attention to marketing opportunities on Pinterest! Realize that when a consumer creates a board on her "dream wedding," you as a maker of wedding dresses, supplier of wedding flowers, or owner of a wedding venue, would love to get your product or service "pinned" to her board as a possible option. Realize that if you, as a knick knack store, create a board called "gift ideas for moms," you can do the hard work of collecting great gift ideas, so that last minute Mother's Day shoppers will use your board to select the gifts that they want, and these items can "live" on your own eCommerce online store.

Once you understand the idea of visual bookmarking or "idea boards," then you've "got" Pinterest.

As on other social media, people can "follow" other people or brands (or just their boards) and when that person, brand, or board has a new pin, that new pin shows in their news feed. In addition, notifications are generated when someone likes, comments, or repins one of your pin (or boards, or account).

Search or Browse Pinterest

People can search Pinterest directly, or by clicking on the categories button, one can browse Pinterest by categories. To do that, simply click on the categories button at the top right of the search screen. Here's a screenshot:

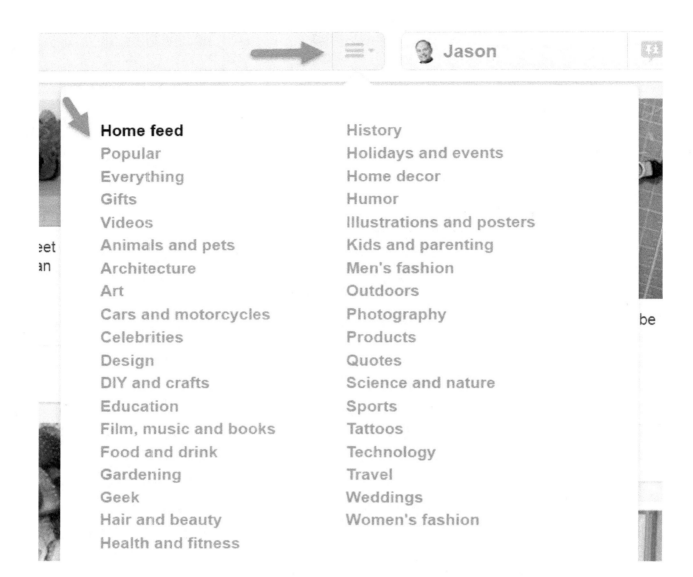

The "home feed," of course, is your news feed on Pinterest: pins selected for you by the Pinterest algorithm based on your previous interests and engagements. The other categories are a way to browse Pinterest by topic, just as you might browse Amazon.

While most of Pinterest is retail-oriented and most of that female-oriented, if you sell to men, do not despair. There are men to be found on Pinterest and topics of interest to men. For example, check out Men's fashion at *http://jmlinks.com/2q* or pet accessories at *http://jmlinks.com/2r*. Classic cars, sporting goods, and other shopping and/or do-it-yourself activities are popular with the male demographic and can be found on Pinterest. Anything connecting to do-it-yourself or recipes / cooking / home decor is also a good bet as a marketing opportunity.

Pinterest has an excellent guide on how to use the platform at *http://jmlinks.com/2s*, an in-depth help center at *http://jmlinks.com/2t,* and a *Pinterest for business center* at *http://jmlinks.com/2u.* Between using these official guides, and systematically researching what's happening on Pinterest, you'll easily see marketing opportunities for your product, service, or company. (*Or, you'll quickly realize that Pinterest is not for you, and you can move on to a more promising social media.*)

▶▶ INVENTORY COMPANIES ON PINTEREST

The best way to research whether Pinterest has any value to your marketing is to research other companies on Pinterest and observe how their fans interact with them on the platform. First, you need to understand how to find companies on Pinterest. Second, you should make a list of companies (and boards) to follow on Pinterest (and follow them with your personal profile). Third, you need to know how to determine what customers are doing on Pinterest, and fourth, you must assess whether any of this has potential value for our company's marketing strategy.

Ways to Search Pinterest

First identify the keyword themes that matter to you and your potential customers. For example, if you are a maker of dog toys, then your targets are people who have dogs and are using Pinterest as a way to brainstorm toys for dogs and interact with other Pinterest users about the pros and cons of specific dog toys. In some cases these will be items to buy, in other cases items to make, and in still others blog posts, infographics, pictures or videos that relate to the theme of "dog toys."

Type the words "dog toys": into the search box while you are logged into Pinterest. Here's a screenshot:

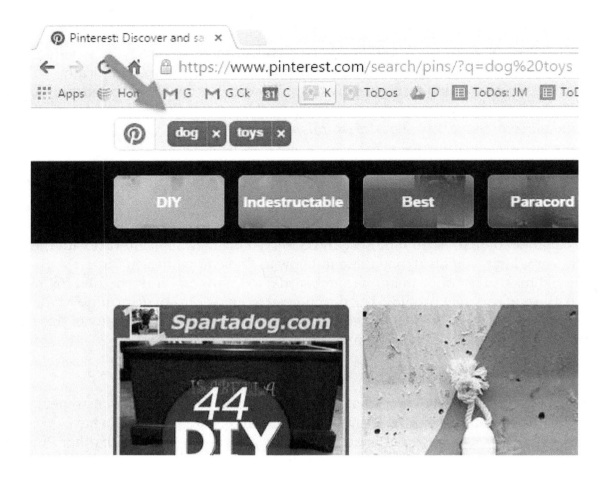

Pinterest, like any search engine, displays results below that have the words "dog toys" in them. If you click on a pin, then you can go down to view that pin and also see the board and/or account associated with that pin. For example, here's a pin that came up when I searched for "dog toys" at *http://jmlinks.com/2v*.

Found on barkpost.com

16 Gifts For Monsters of Destruction Who Will Probably Destroy Their Gifts

🅱 BarkPost

16 pawducts specifically for ruff chewers

If you click on the Pin, you go their website at *http://jmlinks.com/2w*, where (guess what) you can not only **read** about the products, but you can also **buy** them! Back to the pin on Pinterest, on the right hand side you can see the "account" and "board" to which this item has been pinned. Here's a screenshot:

If you click on *Liz Schloegel*, you go up to her account at *http://jmlinks.com/2x* or the board itself by clicking on *Follow board* at *http://jmlinks.com/2y*. Users can like, comment on, or repin pins by clicking into them and then selecting the appropriate button.

Now, Ms. Schloegel, of course, is just an average person, simply pinning and sharing items of interest to her because of her passion for dogs. You are more interested in how competitors and other companies use Pinterest as a marketing vehicle. To find companies, look at the pins returned for your search and at the bottom look for URL's that sound corporate or pins that indicate "promoted pins." For instance, you might end up at any of these companies' Pinterest pages:

> **Waggo Home** (*https://www.pinterest.com/WaggoHome/*) - Lifestyle brand and purveyor of design-driven, happy-centric goodies for home and pet. You'll see that they have a board called "ETC" focused on dogs at *https://www.pinterest.com/WaggoHome/etc/*.

> **Ruff Guides** (*https://www.pinterest.com/source/ruffguides.com/*) – a purveyor of dog-friendly guides to the United States.

> **Collar Planet Online** (*https://www.pinterest.com/collarplanet/*) - specializes in unique Martingale Collars, Pet Jewelry, Jeweled and Leather Dog Collars and Leashes. Large assortment of dog costumes, dog clothes and more!

> **Swanky Pet** (*https://www.pinterest.com/swankypet/*) - Stylish dog collars and more! All items are made-to-order --- let them know what to make for you!

A quick way to find companies after a search is to hit CTRL+F on your keyboard (COMMAND F on Mac) and type in "promoted." That will highlight the promoted (company) pins. These are pins that are being advertised, and consequently will originate from companies as opposed to individuals. As you research companies via your keywords, look for companies with many followers and whose boards / pins show a great deal of interaction: many pins, likes, repins, and comments. Pinterest, after all, is a *social* medium, and your goal is to identify companies that "get" Pinterest well enough to build large, engaged follower communities.

You can also browse Pinterest by category at *https://www.pinterest.com/categories/*. Again, within relevant categories, try to identify companies as opposed to individuals so you can "reverse engineer" their marketing efforts.

Use Google to Search Pinterest

A second way to search Pinterest to find companies of interest is to use Google. Simply go to Google and type in *site:pinterest.com* plus your keywords, as for example: *site:pinterest.com dog toys* at *http://jmlinks.com/2z*. Remember there is *no space* between the colon and *pinterest.com*! Note that at the top of the search results, Google will usually find the Pinterest category page, in this case at *https://www.pinterest.com/explore/dog-toys/*. There, you can drill down to pins, boards, and pages of interest.

A third way is to simply go to competitor websites, or websites of companies you like, and look for the Pinterest icon. Then just click over to Pinterest and follow their company or specific boards of that company. For example, from *http://www.rei.com/*, you'll see the link to their Pinterest page at *https://www.pinterest.com/reicoop/*.

Not surprisingly, since Pinterest is so successful in consumer retail, many of your large retailers have the most sophisticated marketing efforts on Pinterest. Identify a few consumer retailers you like, follow them on Pinterest, and "reverse engineer" their marketing strategies. Here are some of my favorites:

Target at *https://www.pinterest.com/target/*.

Martha Stewart Living at *https://www.pinterest.com/marthastewart/*

Chobani at *https://www.pinterest.com/chobani/*.

Birchbox at *https://www.pinterest.com/birchbox/*.

Everyday Health at *https://www.pinterest.com/everydayhealth/*.

Free People at *https://www.pinterest.com/freepeople/*.

Intel at *https://www.pinterest.com/intel/*.

A Pinterest Trick

It's a little geeky, but you can create a very special type of URL, type this into your browser, and see what pins are being pinned for any given website. For example,

https://www.pinterest.com/source/nytimes.com/ = *pins from the New York Times*

https://www.pinterest.com/source/rei.com = pins from REI.com

You can do this for your own website, as in

https://www.pinterest.com/source/jm-seo.org/ = pins from JM-seo.org.

Simply replace *jm-seo.org* in the string above with your own domain, and then copy/paste the complete URL into the address bar of your browser. Do this for your company on a regular basis (bookmark the URL), and you can see what customers and potential customers are pinning from your website; within Pinterest analytics, you can verify ownership of your website and get even more details on your own site.

This is important because you want to see what types of pins are getting customer interaction on Pinterest. Another method to see what's being shared on Pinterest about a specific domain is to use a tool like Buzzsumo (*http://www.buzzsumo.com/*). Simply type in the domain of interest into Buzzsumo, sort the Pinterest column on the right, and you can see the most popular content on Pinterest for a particular domain.

IDENTIFY COMPANIES WHO DO PINTEREST MARKETING WELL, AND REVERSE ENGINEER THEM

Don't be afraid to "follow" companies via Pinterest (even your competitors). In fact, I strongly encourage it: by "following" companies you actually "like," you'll experience them marketing to you, and you can then reverse engineer this for your own company.

For your first TODO, download the **Pinterest Research Worksheet**. For the worksheet, go to *https://www.jm-seo.org/workbooks* (click on Pinterest, enter the code 'pinterest2016' to register if you have not already done so), and click on the link to the "Pinterest Research Worksheet." You'll answer questions as to whether your potential customers are on Pinterest, identify brands to follow, and inventory what you like and dislike about their Pinterest set up and marketing strategy.

» SET UP AND OPTIMIZE YOUR PINTEREST PAGE

Now that you've got the basics of Pinterest down, it's time to set up or optimize your Pinterest page. Remember, people have "profiles" and businesses have "accounts" on Pinterest, often also called "Pages." You'll generally want a business account, or Page, on Pinterest. To set one up for the first time, go to *Pinterest for Business* at *https://business.pinterest.com/*. You can also convert a "profile" to a business "account" if you mistakenly joined as an individual at *https://business.pinterest.com/*.

Once you've joined, you have only a very basic set up – your profile picture, username (URL), "about you," location, and website. That's it. Once you've filled out this information, you're set up on Pinterest as a business.

Next, set up some boards by clicking on the "Create a Board" on the left of the screen. Here's a screenshot:

When you create a board, give it a name, a description, a category, a map or location (useful if you are a local business). If you're just building out the board, you can also temporarily make it *secret* and then change it to *public* at a later date.

If you want to make a board collaborative, you identify "collaborators" by typing in their names or email addresses. Pinterest will then invite them to start pinning items to your board. The easiest way to start pinning items to your board is to download the "Pinterest button" onto your browser. You can also manually copy URL's over to pin an item. With the concept that a board is an "idea board," start identifying and pinning items from the Web such as blog posts, images or photos, and yes, even products from your eCommerce store to your new board.

Board Strategy

Social media is a party, not a prison. Your board should attract people to follow it by providing something useful, something visual, something fun. Ask these questions. What is the board "about"? Who will want to "follow" it, Pin stuff from it (or to it), comment, share, and click from the board to your products. Take a board like "Gifts for

Dog Lovers" at *http://jmlinks.com/3a* vs. the board "Dog Gifs" at *http://jmlinks.com/3b*. The purpose of the former is to identify fun dog gifts to BUY, while the purpose of the latter is to share funny pictures of dogs and build the brand image of *BarkPost* (*http://barkpost.com/*), a New York-based blog on dogs that also sells dog-related products. Both are legitimate social media marketing users of Pinterest – the former is just a more direct plea to "buy our stuff," whereas the latter is more a "look at this cool stuff" (and by the way check out all the cool stuff we sell).

> *Hard sell* or *soft sell*: both work on Pinterest.

In sum, it is incredibly important to brainstorm your boards! The questions are:

- **What is this board about?** What ideas does it collect, how does it function as a useful "idea-generator" on a particular topic?
- **Who will be interested in this board?** What value are you providing as the board-creator and board-curator by having this board? A board on dog toy ideas "saves time" for people who a) love dogs and want toys and/or b) need to buy a gift for a person who loves dogs and wants toys. Your value is curating "in" the cool stuff, and curating "out" the dumb stuff. A board that collects funny pictures of dogs is meant to give viewers a quick and easy way to get a few laughs during their busy day, and a board that collects do-it-yourself ideas for cheap dog toys helps dog lovers save money, and have fun, by building their own dog toys. Who will be interested is a function of what the board is about.
- **What will you pin to this board, and where does that content live?** Is it stuff from your eCommerce store? Stuff on Amazon? Blog posts, or how to articles? Items from your own blog? YouTube video? Content is king, on Pinterest, as on all social media.

For your second **TODO**, download the **Pinterest Setup Worksheet**. For the worksheet, go to *https://www.jm-seo.org/workbooks* (click on Pinterest, enter the code 'pinterest2016' to register if you have not already done so), and click on the link to the "Pinterest Setup Worksheet." You'll answer and outline the basic setup issues for your Pinterest business account (page) and boards.

» BRAINSTORM AND EXECUTE A PINNING STRATEGY

Content is king, and queen, and jack. Now that you've set up your Pinterest Page, you need to think about posting (or rather pinning). Turn back to your Content Marketing plan, and remember you'll need both other people's content and your own content to pin:

- **Photographs and Images**. Pinterest is very visual, and you'll need to systematically identify photographs and images that fit with your brand message and ideally encourage likes, comments, and repins (shares).
- **Blog Post and Content Summaries**. To the extent that you have an active blog and are posting items that fit with the common uses of Pinterest, pin your blog posts to Pinterest.
    - Note that the first or "featured" image will become the shareable image. Choose striking, fun images for your pins, even if what you are pinning is just a blog post!
- **Quotes**. People love quotes, and taking memorable quotes and pasting them on graphics is a win/win.
- **Infographics and Instructographics**. Factoids, how to articles, especially ones that are fun, do-it-yourself articles, lists or collections of tips or products, are excellent for Pinterest. Anything that helps a person organize ideas about products or services to buy or make will work well on Pinterest.
- **Quizzes, Surveys, and Response-provoking posts**. Ask a question, and get an answer or more. Great for encouraging interactivity. Use a board to actively ask for collaboration; a board on do-it-yourself dog toys is a natural way to ask your fans to participate.
- **Items to Buy**. Yes! You can (and should) pin items to buy on your Pinterest boards. Unlike most other social media users, Pinterest users are "in" the shopping mode in many ways, so tastefully pinning cool items that can be bought is not just expected but encouraged.

Indeed, Pinterest realizes that buying is a logical way to monetize the site, and so they have announced "Buy it on Pinterest" at *https://about.pinterest.com/en/buy-it*. You can also read about *buyable pins* at *http://jmlinks.com/3d*. Another option here is so-called *rich pins*, which are dynamically updated pins from your eCommerce store. Learn about them at *http://jmlinks.com/3e*.

Clearly, Pinterest will help you shamelessly promote, link to, and sell your stuff via Pinterest! In this sense it is unique among social media in being so unabashedly pro-ecommerce.

Once you've set up your Pinterest business account, and begun to populate it with boards and pins on a regular basis, you've essentially "set up" the party. Now it's time to send out the invitations. In and of itself, neither a Pinterest Page nor a Pinterest board will be self-promoting!

MAKE YOUR BOARDS USEFUL, FUN, AND MESMERIZING FOR YOUR USERS

Remember: social media is a **party**. You must have yummy yummy food and entertainment for people to show up, and stick around. So as you promote your Pinterest Page, always keep front and center "what's in it for them" – what will they get by "following" your Pinterest page and/or Pinterest boards, and checking them out on a regular basis?

Assuming your Page and/or boards have lots of useful, provocative content, here are some common ways to promote your Pinterest account and boards:

- **Real World to Social.** Don't forget the real world! If you are a museum store, for example, be sure that the cashiers recommend to people that they "follow" your Pinterest Page and/or boards? *Why? Because they'll get insider tips, fun do-it-yourself posts, announcements on upcoming museum and museum store events, selected items from your online museum store, etc. Oh, and we'll share collections of do-it-yourself tips as well as gift ideas for that hard-to-buy-for someone in your life.*
- **Cross-Promotion**. Link your website to your Pinterest Page, your blog posts to your Pinterest Page, your Twitter to your Pinterest Page, etc. Notice how big brands like REI do this: one digital property promotes another digital property.
- **Email**. Email your customer list and ask them to "follow" your Page or boards. Be specific: you can drill down to specific subgroups and match their interests with specific boards. Again, you must have a reason why they'll follow it: what's in it for them? Have a contest, give away something for free, or otherwise motivate them to click from the email to your Page, and then "follow" your page or board.

- **Pinterest Internal**. Interact with other Pages, Pins, and Boards, repin their content, comment on timely topics using #hashtags, and reach out to complementary Pages to work with you on co-promotion.
- **Pinterest SEO / Search**. People use Pinterest to generate ideas, especially before shopping for something big like a wedding or a dorm room, and therefore search is very big on Pinterest. Research your keywords and name your boards and pins after those keywords, and include keywords in your description. As you get likes, pins, and repins, the Pinterest algorithm will rewards your pins with higher placement in Pinterest search results.
- **Use Pinterest Plugins**. Pinterest has numerous plugins that allow you to "embed" your Pinterest items on your website, and allow users to easily "pin" your eCommerce or blog posts to their own boards. Get it at *https://wordpress.org/plugins/pinterest-pin-it-button/*. In this way, your blog can promote your Pinterest Page, your eCommerce site can promote your Pinterest Page, and your Pinterest Page can promote your eCommerce store and/or blog. Similarly, your YouTube videos can promote your Pinterest Page, and your Pinterest Page can promote your YouTube Videos. And the same goes, of course, for your Pinterest boards.
- **Leverage your Fans**. People who like your Page are your best promoters. Remember, it's *social* (!) media, and encouraging your customers to share your content is the name of the game. You want to leverage your fans as much as possible to share your content. Asking key influencers to participate in a board is a great way to both build content and encourage publicity.

ENCOURAGE YOUR FANS TO CONTRIBUTE TO YOUR BOARDS, AND SHARE YOUR CONTENT

Here are some specific items worth mentioning:

Group boards. Group boards allow you to collaborate with your employees and customers on Pinterest. Check them out at *http://jmlinks.com/3c*. Brainstorm a collaborative project between you and your customers, and use Pinterest as a means to cooperate online.

Rich Pins and "Buy it" Pins. These two mechanisms link your eCommerce store to/from Pinterest. They are not promotion mechanisms per se, but they make the buying process as easy as possible. Check out the links at *http://jmlinks.com/3d* and *http://jmlinks.com/3e* to learn more about these cross-linking strategies.

Hashtags. Like Twitter, Pinterest has hashtags which are ways that people can communicate on a theme. Anything marked with a #hashtag is clickable in a pin. Here's a screenshot of a pin with the hashtag #weddingdresses highlighted:

And here's what happens if you click on that link: *https://www.pinterest.com/search?q=weddingdress*. It generates a search on Pinterest for wedding dress with a little ambiguity about the space. So the long and short of it is that by including hashtags in your pins, you become more findable in Pinterest search whether directly or by the search engine function. Identify relevant hashtags and include them in your best pins.

Search. Throughout, remember that search is very important on Pinterest. Make sure that you know your keywords, and that you weave these keywords into the titles and descriptions of your pins and boards. People use Pinterest as a "search engine" to find interesting products and ideas, similar to how people use Yelp to identify fun restaurants and great plumbers.

> *Search, and therefore search optimization, should be a major part of your Pinterest promotion strategy.*

Advertise. Advertising is increasingly important to success on Pinterest. I've mentioned rich pins and "buy it" pins, which are integrations between your online store and Pinterest. "Promoted pins" function much the same way as "promoted posts" on Facebook: you identify a pin to promote, and by advertising, Pinterest pushes these pins to the top of the news feed and search functions on the site. Learn more at *https://ads.pinterest.com/*.

≫ MEASURE YOUR RESULTS

Once you set up a business account and boards on Pinterest, Pinterest gives you decent metrics on how popular they are. To find them, click on the gear icon beneath your profile picture at the right. Here's a screenshot:

That will transport you to *https://analytics.pinterest.com/*. You can also confirm your website and Pinterest will show you what people are pinning from your website or blog.

Google Analytics

For many of us, we want to drive traffic from Pinterest to our website, even to our ecommerce store or to download a free eBook or software package to get a sales lead. Sign up for Google Analytics (*https://www.google.com/analytics*) and install the required tracking code. Inside of your Google Analytics account on the left column, drill down by clicking on Acquisition > Social > Overview. Then on the right hand side of the screen you'll see a list of Social Networks. Find Pinterest on that list, and click on that. Google Analytics will tell you what URLs people clicked to from Pinterest to your Website, giving you insights into what types of web content people find attractive.

You can also create a custom Advanced Segment to look at only Pinterest traffic and its behavior. For information on how to create custom Advanced Segments in Google Analytics, go to *http://jmlinks.com/1f*. For the Google help files on Advanced Segments go to *http://jmlinks.com/1g*.

In sum, inside of Pinterest you can see how people interact with your Page and posts. Inside of Google Analytics, you can see where they land on your website and what they do after they arrive. This includes eCommerce, as Google Analytics is very well integrated with eCommerce. You can learn not only if Pinterest is sending traffic to your website but also whether that traffic is converting to inquiries, downloads, and eCommerce sales.

» DELIVERABLE: A PINTEREST MARKETING PLAN

Now that we've come to the end of our chapter on Pinterest, your DELIVERABLE has arrived. For the worksheet, go to *https://www.jm-seo.org/workbooks* (click on Pinterest, enter the code 'pinterest2016' to register if you have not already done so), and click on the link to the "Pinterest Marketing Plan." By filling out this plan, you and your team will establish a vision of what you want to achieve via Pinterest.

» TOP TEN PINTEREST MARKETING TOOLS AND RESOURCES

Here are the top ten tools and resources to help you with Pinterest marketing. For an up-to-date list, go to *https://www.jm-seo.org/workbooks* (click on Pinterest, enter the code 'pinterest2016' to register if you have not already done so), and click on the link to the *Social Media Toolbook* link, and drill down to the Pinterest chapter.

PINTEREST GOODIES - https://about.pinterest.com/goodies

> Made more for the end user than the business user, this is a resource by Pinterest about Pinterest. For example, both the iOS and Android apps are available here. Don't miss the 'Pin It' button which makes it easy to pin content from your browser, as well as widgets for your website to encourage Pinterest.
>
> **Rating:** 4 Stars | **Category:** tool

PINTEREST PIN IT BUTTON - https://business.pinterest.com/pin-it-button

Want your business to be discovered on Pinterest? The Pin It button allows your customers to save what they like to Pinterest and shows their followers what they're interested in. An easy way to get referral traffic and what Pinterest calls, 'a button that works for you'.

Rating: 4 Stars | **Category:** tool

PINTEREST RICH PINS - https://business.pinterest.com/rich-pins

Rich Pins are pins that include extra information on the pin itself. The six types of rich pins are: app, movie, recipe, article, product, and place. Use these six rich pins in addition to your 'pin it' link to further enhance your post for your viewers.

Rating: 4 Stars | **Category:** tool

PINTEREST TOOLS FOR BUSINESS - https://business.pinterest.com/tools

Yes, you wanted it. Yes, they created it: a one-stop resource of tools to help your business succeed on Pinterest. Has not only official Pinterest tools, but also a compilation of third party business-friendly tools to help you pin it, to win it.

Rating: 4 Stars | **Category:** tool

IFTTT - https://ifttt.com

This app, If Then Then That, is a great tool for linking multiple social media accounts. It allows you to create 'recipes' that link your tools exactly the way you like them! For example: make a recipe that adds to a Google Apps spreadsheet every time a particular user uploads to Instagram - a great way to keep up with your competitors SMM strategies! With over 120 supported applications, the 'recipes' are endless, making this a good tool for your SMM strategies.

Rating: 4 Stars | **Category:** tool

POSTRIS - http://postris.com

An advanced, web-based Instagram dashboard for tracking and organizing your Instagram account and daily updates from leading publications and social networks. Helps users keep up with what is trending on Instagram

Rating: 3 Stars | **Category:** tool

LOVELIST - http://lovelistapp.com

> This iPhone app lets you scan any barcode and create a pin of the product instantly, to pin all the products in your product line easily, or like a wedding registry scanner to create a wish list.

> **Rating:** 3 Stars | **Category:** tool

PINGROUPIE - http://pingroupie.com

> Use this tool to find group boards on Pinterest where you can join and contribute. Additionally, PinGroupie has options for sorting boards by popularity so you can quickly see those with the biggest following, or most pins or likes.

> **Rating:** 3 Stars | **Category:** tool

CANVA - https://canva.com

> This free image editing tool is optimized for Pinterest so all of your pins and boards look sleek. Also has an iPad app.

> **Rating:** 3 Stars | **Category:** tool

PINTEREST WIDGET BUILDER - https://business.pinterest.com/widget-builder

> This tool allows users to further integrate Pinterest into their website by allowing you to build a 'Pin It' button, a 'Follow' button and other Pinterest widgets.

> **Rating:** 3 Stars | **Category:** tool

3

PINTEREST TOOLS

As a social and visual bookmarking system, Pinterest has a cornucopia of free resources and free tools to make your life easier. Below I produce my favorite tools and resources (in rank order). Remember that by registering your copy of the workbook, you can access the *Social Media Toolbook*, which has all the tools in convenient, clickable PDF format. To register, go to *https://www.jm-seo.org/workbooks* (click on Pinterest, enter the code 'pinterest2016' to register if you have not already done so), and click on the link to the *Social Media Toolbook*.

Here are free Pinterest tools and resources, sorted with the best items first.

PINTEREST ANALYTICS - https://business.pinterest.com/pinterest-analytics

> Use this tool to easily see what people like from your Pinterest profile and what they pin from your website. Learn about your audience by viewing metrics and common interests. Great tool to analyze your Pinterest marketing strategy.
>
> **Rating:** 4 Stars | **Category:** tool

PINTEREST GOODIES - https://about.pinterest.com/goodies

> Made more for the end user than the business user, this is a resource by Pinterest about Pinterest. For example, both the iOS and Android apps are available here. Don't miss the 'Pin It' button which makes it easy to pin content from your browser, as well as widgets for your website to encourage Pinterest.
>
> **Rating:** 4 Stars | **Category:** tool

PINTEREST PIN IT BUTTON - https://business.pinterest.com/pin-it-button

Want your business to be discovered on Pinterest? The Pin It button allows your customers to save what they like to Pinterest and shows their followers what they're interested in. An easy way to get referral traffic and what Pinterest calls, 'a button that works for you'.

Rating: 4 Stars | **Category:** tool

PINTEREST RICH PINS - https://business.pinterest.com/rich-pins

Rich Pins are pins that include extra information on the pin itself. The six types of rich pins are: app, movie, recipe, article, product, and place. Use these six rich pins in addition to your 'pin it' link to further enhance your post for your viewers.

Rating: 4 Stars | **Category:** tool

PINTEREST TOOLS FOR BUSINESS - https://business.pinterest.com/tools

Yes, you wanted it. Yes, they created it: a one-stop resource of tools to help your business succeed on Pinterest. Has not only official Pinterest tools, but also a compilation of third party business-friendly tools to help you pin it, to win it.

Rating: 4 Stars | **Category:** tool

IFTTT - https://ifttt.com

This app, If Then Then That, is a great tool for linking multiple social media accounts. It allows you to create 'recipes' that link your tools exactly the way you like them! For example: make a recipe that adds to a Google Apps spreadsheet every time a particular user uploads to Instagram - a great way to keep up with your competitors SMM strategies! With over 120 supported applications, the 'recipes' are endless, making this a good tool for your SMM strategies.

Rating: 4 Stars | **Category:** tool

POSTRIS - http://postris.com

An advanced, web-based Instagram dashboard for tracking and organizing your Instagram account and daily updates from leading publications and social networks. Helps users keep up with what is trending on Instagram

Rating: 3 Stars | **Category:** tool

THE RETAILERS GUIDE TO PINTEREST -
http://www.business2community.com/pinterest/retailers-guide-pinterest-01016672

> Business2community.com shares this short yet informative 'how to' article on what to do when, where, how, and why on Pinterest as a business.
>
> **Rating:** 3 Stars | **Category:** article

PINTEREST FOR BUSINESS - http://www.businessnewsdaily.com/7552-pinterest-business-guide.html

> Pinterest can be used to promote your business, especially if you reach one of the two intertwined demographics: young women and shoppers. This brief but meaty article explains how.
>
> **Rating:** 3 Stars | **Category:** archive

ULTIMATE PINTEREST MARKETING GUIDE - https://blog.kissmetrics.com/ultimate-pinterest-marketing-guide/

> KISSmetrics has produced a landmark guide to how to use Pinterest for business. It's a great, basic read for the beginner.
>
> **Rating:** 3 Stars | **Category:** article

LoveList - http://lovelistapp.com

> This iPhone app lets you scan any barcode and create a pin of the product instantly, to pin all the products in your product line easily, or like a wedding registry scanner to create a wish list.
>
> **Rating:** 3 Stars | **Category:** tool

PINTEREST FOR BUSINESS NEWSLETTER - https://business.pinterest.com/contact-us

> Love Pinterest? Want to love Pinterest? Want to learn to love Pinterest? They'll help you with their lively and self-promotional Pinterest for business newsletter. Get the inside scoop on Pinterest by Pinterest (for business users).
>
> **Rating:** 3 Stars | **Category:** eletter

PinGroupie - http://pingroupie.com

Use this tool to find group boards on Pinterest where you can join and contribute. Additionally, PinGroupie has options for sorting boards by popularity so you can quickly see those with the biggest following, or most pins or likes.

Rating: 3 Stars | **Category:** tool

CANVA - https://canva.com

This free image editing tool is optimized for Pinterest so all of your pins and boards look sleek. Also has an iPad app.

Rating: 3 Stars | **Category:** tool

PINTEREST HELP TOPICS - https://help.pinterest.com/articles

Browse topic by topic through the Pinterest help pages. For example, learn the basics of what pins are and how to use them. Great for beginners.

Rating: 3 Stars | **Category:** resource

PINTEREST FOR BUSINESS - https://business.pinterest.com

Looking to 'get started' on Pinterest? Here is the official site on how a business page for Pinterest works.

Rating: 3 Stars | **Category:** resource

PINTEREST BUSINESS GUIDES - https://business.pinterest.com/pinterest-guides

Downloadable business-friendly guides from Pinterest about how to use Pinterest effectively for your business.

Rating: 3 Stars | **Category:** resource

PINTEREST HELP CENTER - https://help.pinterest.com

Need help? Well, guess what, Pinterest has a robust help section, mainly for users but useful for you as a business marketer. You gotta know how they use it, to use it to market to them!

Rating: 3 Stars | **Category:** resource

PINTEREST WIDGET BUILDER - https://business.pinterest.com/widget-builde

This tool allows users to further integrate Pinterest into their website by allowing you to build a 'Pin It' button, a 'Follow' button and other Pinterest widgets.

Rating: 3 Stars | **Category:** tool

PINSTAMATIC - http://pinstamatic.com

This free tool can be used to quickly create visual content for Pinterest boards without any editing tools. Use it to add a website snapshot, quotes and text, sticky notes, Twitter profile, calendar date, location map, captioned photo, and even a Spotify track.

Rating: 3 Stars | **Category:** tool

PINALERTS - http://pinalerts.com

Pinalerts allows you to receive email notifications whenever someone pins something from your website.

Rating: 2 Stars | **Category:** tool

PINVOLVE - http://pinvolve.co

This tool automatically syncs your Facebook and Pinterest pages, allowing you to integrate your social media marketing strategies. Free for one Facebook page with limited pinning.

Rating: 2 Stars | **Category:** tool

VIRALTAG - http://viraltag.com

Use this tool to plan and publish visual content to social media platforms. This is a great tool for managing multiple social media platforms at once and is is free for three social profiles.

Rating: 2 Stars | **Category:** tool

VIRALWOOT - http://viralwoot.com

This tool helps increase your Pinterest visibility by monitoring your Pinterest profile and pins. You can promote your pins and create pinalerts!

Rating: 2 Stars | **Category:** tool

PINTEREST FACEBOOK PAGE TAB - http://woobox.com/pinterest

This tool allows you to add a Pinterest tab to your Facebook page; another great way to integrate your social media marketing strategies! Get complete stats for page views, visits, and likes, segmented by fans and non-fans who view your Facebook page tab.

Rating: 2 Stars | **Category:** tool

PINTEREST BRAND GUIDELINES - https://business.pinterest.com/brand-guidelines

New to Pinterest? This set of guidelines will help any business use the Pinterest brand in their marketing. It includes information on the logo, badge, and what words or phrases are going to be most helpful and most appropriate for your marketing needs.

Rating: 2 Stars | **Category:** resource

TAILWIND - https://tailwindapp.com

This tool provides Pinterest analytics. Users can view total pins, repins, likes, followers and a graph of your score as well as schedule pins. Additionally, users can view influential followers.

Rating: 2 Stars | **Category:** tool

PIN SEARCH - https://chrome.google.com/webstore/detail/pin-search-image-search-o/okiaciimfpgbpdhnfdllhdkicpmdoakm

An extension for Chrome browser that allows users to easily find related photos and information for photos posted on Pinterest.

Rating: 2 Stars | **Category:** service

PINTEREST BLOG - https://business.pinterest.com/blog

The official blog by Pinterest about Pinterest, targeted at small businesses.

Rating: 2 Stars | **Category:** blog